D0538423

THE CALIFORNIA GOLD RUSH

Miners at Foster's Bar in California search for gold with a series of sluices, in this 1851 illustration.

THE CALIFORNIA GOLD RUSH

◆

BARBARA SAFFER

◆

MASO.   LISHERS

Mason Crest Publishers
370 Reed Road
Broomall PA 19008

First printing

1 3 5 7 9 8 6 4 2

Library of Congress Cataloging-in-Publication Data
on file at the Library of Congress

ISBN 1-59084-060-7

Publisher's note: many of the quotations in this book come from
original sources, and contain the spelling and grammatical
inconsistencies of the original text.

CONTENTS

Sutter's Mill was the famed site where gold was initially spotted. Once the secret escaped, people from all over the world flocked to California to find their fortune. Today, this site is the city of Sacramento.

GOLD, GOLD, GOLD!

Sutter came to America. He hoped to escape from financial problems, and left his wife and four children behind in Switzerland. While working as a trader in the New World, Sutter heard that Upper California—then a province of Mexico—had a mild climate, fertile soil, and available land. Sutter made his way to California in 1839, became a Mexican citizen, and was granted 50,000 acres of land in the central valley, near the junction of the Sacramento and American Rivers.

Over the next few years, Sutter prospered. With the help of Indian workers, he built a fort that contained blacksmith and carpentry shops, a tannery, a gristmill, a blanket-weaving shop, and a distillery. He grew wheat and other grains, tended an orchard filled with apple, peach, olive, almond,

John Sutter acquired a large area of California land from Mexico in 1839. Nine years later, gold was discovered on his property. Though some people struck it rich during the California Gold Rush, Sutter was forced off his land and into bankruptcy.

pear, and fig trees, raised two acres of roses, and acquired 13,000 head of cattle. Sutter called his ranch New Helvetia in honor of Switzerland, whose Latin name is Helvetia. Other people called it Sutter's Fort.

Sutter's Fort, which later became the city of Sacramento, was a stopping place for Americans migrating from the United States to northern California. Sutter gave travelers food and water and offered them jobs as blacksmiths, carpenters, threshers, clerks, wagon drivers, hide tanners, and crewmen on his riverboat. As Sutter expanded his operations, he needed more lumber for buildings. In the summer of 1847, Sutter hired a carpenter named James Marshall to build and operate a sawmill in New Helvetia. Marshall took his crew up the American River to Coloma, in the foothills of the Sierra Nevada Mountains, and began construction. By early 1848, Sutter's Mill was nearly complete.

On January 24, 1848, as Marshall was checking the sawmill's **tailrace** (the channel that carried water away from the mill), he noticed small chunks of yellow metal. "My eye was caught with the glimpse of something shining in the bottom of the ditch," he later said. "There was about a foot of water running then. I reached my hand down and picked it up; it made my heart thump, for I was certain it was gold."

Marshall pounded one chunk with a rock, and it flattened easily, like gold. To make sure the shiny lumps were not "fool's gold" (iron pyrite), Marshall took them to Jenny Wimmer, the camp cook. Wimmer knew how to test for gold. She tossed several of the chunks into a kettle of boiling lye soap, which dissolves many things, but not gold. The next day Wimmer poured out the soap, and the yellow lumps lay unharmed at the bottom of the kettle.

For forty-niners, the term that best described the gold rush was "seeing the elephant." The expression came from a story about a circus elephant. In the tale, a farmer, hearing a circus was in town, filled his wagon with eggs and vegetables for the market there. The farmer had never observed an elephant and was very anxious to see one. On the way to town, the farmer met the circus parade, led by an elephant. The farmer was thrilled, but his horses were terrified. Fleeing, the horses overturned the wagon, scattering eggs and vegetables everywhere. "I don't give a hang," said the farmer. "I have seen the elephant." Gold hunters often said they were off to "see the elephant," meaning they were ready to endure any hardship for the opportunity of a lifetime.

In the last issue of a San Francisco newspaper, *The Californian*, publisher B. R. Buckelew wrote: "The majority of our subscribers and many of our advertisers have closed their doors and places of business and left town…The whole country, from San Francisco to Los Angeles, and from the seashore to the Sierra Nevada, resounds to the sordid cry of Gold! Gold! Gold!"

On January 28, Marshall rode 36 miles through pouring rain, burst into Sutter's home, and showed him the chunks of yellow metal. Sutter and Marshall looked up the properties of gold in an encyclopedia and tested the lumps once again. They pounded them, weighed them in water, and treated them with acid to see if they dissolved. Without a doubt, Marshall had discovered gold!

John Sutter wrote the following in his diary, "He was soaked to the skin and dripping water. He told me he had something of the utmost importance to tell me, that he wanted to speak to me in private…We went upstairs to the next floor, and, although there was no one in the house except the bookkeeper, he insisted so strongly that we locked ourselves in a room."

Sutter was shaken by the discovery of gold on his land. He knew the treasure would attract hordes of people. He also knew his claim to New Helvetia was in doubt.

For years, American settlers in California had been clamoring for independence from Mexico. For this and other reasons, war broke out between the United States and Mexico in 1846.

The Treaty of Guadalupe Hidalgo, which ended the Mexican War in early 1848, gave California to the United States. Sutter feared the United States would refuse to honor Mexico's land grant, and would take his property.

To gain time, Sutter asked Marshall and his crew to keep the discovery of gold secret for six weeks. During that time, Sutter made a treaty with the Indians—supposedly now the land's owners—for exclusive rights to mine the gold for three years. Sutter also asked the American governor of California, Colonel Richard Barnes Mason, for water and mineral rights to New Helvetia. Mason refused, saying he had no power to make land grants.

Sutter's efforts to retain control of his property failed, and New Helvetia was soon invaded by gold-hunters. In fact, the first gold miners were Sutter's employees,

James Marshall 👉 discovered the gold on Sutter's land. His 1848 find encouraged large numbers of hopeful prospectors to make their way West. Though Marshall gained fame, he never gained a fortune from his find.

who quit their jobs to search for treasure. Only the Indians, who had little desire for gold, stayed to care for Sutter's fields and herds.

The discovery of gold at Sutter's Mill did not remain secret for long. Sutter's workers told people about it, and Sutter himself mentioned it in a letter to a friend. One man, Sam Brannan, was especially eager to spread the news. Brannan—who owned a store close to Sutter's Fort—wanted to lure miners to California, so he could sell them supplies. To further his goal, Brannan carried a bottle of gold dust to San Francisco. There, he hurried up and down the street shouting, "Gold! Gold from the American River!"

Brannan's visit electrified the residents of San Francisco. Every able-bodied citizen—including blacksmiths, clergymen, doctors, journalists, lawyers, soldiers, tailors, schoolteachers, shopkeepers, and lawmen—dropped everything and hastened to the gold fields. Sailors deserted their ships in San Francisco harbor, and joined the treasure hunt. Two San Francisco newspapers soon closed, for lack of employees and readers.

As news of the gold spread, people from all over the world stampeded to the gold fields. California came to be called "El Dorado"—the name was taken from old Spanish legends about a South American kingdom overflowing with gold and jewels. The gold rush made Sam Brannan a wealthy man. John Sutter, however, was ruined. Miners overran New Helvetia, dug up Sutter's land to search for gold, and killed his cattle for food. Years later, when the U.S. Supreme Court upheld Sutter's claim to the land, he had nothing left after paying his debts.

James Marshall also came to a sad end. He joined in the search for gold, but never struck it rich. Eventually, he lost his mind, coming to believe the gold in California was rightfully his. In 1885, Marshall died in a cabin in Coloma, in complete poverty.

GETTING TO CALIFORNIA

CALIFORNIA'S EXTENSIVE GOLD DEPOSITS, DISCOVERED IN 1848, TOUCHED OFF THE WORLD'S first gold rush. In 1849 alone, almost 90,000 people from all over the world hurried to the hills and rivers of California to seek their fortunes. The treasure hunters were called forty-niners, for the first year of the great migration.

Until 1849, California had been a sparsely populated Mexican colony with scattered Indian villages and a few coastal towns. Many of California's residents were "*Californios*"— Mexicans who had lived there for generations.

The first gold miners were residents of California and surrounding areas. News about the gold spread slowly, and when it finally reached the East, people did not believe it. Then, on December 5, 1848, President James K. Polk, who wanted the United States to stretch from coast to coast, told

One of the simplest methods of gold mining involved panning the rivers for nuggets. This method required patience: a grueling day's work often produced little or no gold.

This sketch by a San Francisco resident, made in 1849, shows the city's harbor choked with abandoned ships. Many of the forty-niners traveled to California by ship; when they reached San Francisco, in many cases both passengers and crew left their vessels and went off to search for gold.

Congress, "The accounts of the abundance of gold in California Territory…would scarcely command belief." Polk's announcement fired up the nation. People across the country—almost all men at first—left their jobs and farms, packed their bags, and headed west. The gold rush was on!

To help plan their quest for gold, forty-niners snapped up guidebooks as fast as they could be printed. The books—generally written by people who had never been to California—were loaded with advice about where to go, when to get there, and how to find and collect gold. Two of the most popular guide books were *California and the Way to Get There: With the Official Documents Relating to the Gold Region* and *The **Emigrant's** Guide to California*.

General William Tecumseh Sherman, stationed in California during 1848, wrote: "Stories reached us of fabulous discoveries, and spread throughout the land. Everybody was talking of "Gold! Gold!" until it assumed the character of a fever. Some of our soldiers began to desert."

The gold-rushers also bought heaps of supplies, including red flannel shirts, high boots, wide hats, corduroy pants, pots, pans, kettles, cups, knives, forks, spoons, pickaxes, shovels, spades, hoes, axes, hatchets, daggers, Bowie knives, rifles, pistols, inflatable rubber beds, boats, tents, and bottles of medicine to cure every kind of disease. Forty-niners also purchased all types of mining gear, such as **dredges**, devices to sift and wash gold, ore mills, gadgets that separate gold from rocks using chemicals, and diving suits for collecting gold from stream bottoms. Much of this equipment was too heavy to transport easily, and had to be discarded on the way to the gold fields.

By 1849, people from all over the world—Asia, Australia, Europe, Hawaii, North America, and South America—were scrambling to California. Many came not only to seek their fortunes, but also to find a better way of life. Of the almost

Hiram Pierce, a gold-hunter from Troy, New York, closed his blacksmith shop and left his wife and seven children to go to California via Panama. While stranded in Panama City, he wrote: "There are perhaps 2,000 Americans now on the Isthmus. The prospect of getting away looks very dubious…there are many here that have used up their means, some by gambling and some in other ways, so that they cannot get away. Yet we hope for the best. I think of that shop in Troy, and that wife whose likeness [picture] I look upon and those dear children, and my feelings by some might not be called manly."

When he was finally aboard a ship to San Francisco, Hiram Pierce wrote: "Our mode of living is truly brutish. [At mealtimes] we form ourselves into two lines when we can, on that small part of the deck that is left clear. And a man passes through with the coffee. Another with the sugar. Another with a basket of bread. Another with a bottle of vinegar and molasses. And then the grabbing commences. We catch a piece of meat in the fingers and crowd like a lot of swine, the ship perhaps so careened that you will need to hold on or stagger and pitch like a drunken man. Many behave so swinish that I prefer to stay away unless driven to it by hunger."

90,000 people who hastened to the gold fields in 1849, about 23,000 were not United States citizens.

Gold hunters could get to California by land or sea. Emigrants from America's eastern seaboard generally traveled by ship. Two ocean routes were available. One was down the Atlantic Coast, around Cape Horn at the tip of South America, and up the Pacific Coast to San Francisco. This route, about

17,000 miles, took from four to nine months. The other route was a sea voyage to Central America, an overland journey across the Isthmus of Panama to the Pacific Ocean, and another ship up the Pacific Coast to San Francisco. This trip, close to 6,000 miles, normally took about two to three months. Voyagers on ships were called **argonauts**, after the heroes in Greek mythology who sailed on the ship *Argo* to seek the Golden Fleece.

With tens of thousands of people anxious to get to California, numerous ships were suddenly needed. Broken-down old vessels that had been abandoned years before were dragged out, patched up, and sent to sea jammed with argonauts.

At the beginning of the gold rush, the preferred ocean route was around Cape Horn. The trip, however, was brutal. Passengers broiled near the equator and froze near the Antarctic. Living quarters aboard ship were dirty, smelly, and crowded. Gold-rushers slept on wooden berths, usually three men per bunk, on platforms that were stacked one above the other. Meals aboard ship were dreadful. Without refrigeration, the meats—salt pork and dried beef—rotted, the biscuits became moldy, and the beans were infested with bugs. Fresh produce spoiled and had to be thrown away. Some meals consisted of biscuits, meat, and beans; others consisted of salted fish, bread, and potatoes. There were also frequent servings of lobscouse—a hash made of salt pork, onions, and biscuits. Passengers complained that there were "two bugs for every bean" and "bad coffee, dirty sugar, and wormy bread."

Drinking water, stored in barrels for months, developed a vile taste, and had to be mixed with vinegar and molasses to be drinkable. Moreover, the lack of fruits and vegetables resulted in **scurvy**, a disabling disease caused by lack of vitamin C. People became weak, with swollen gums, loose teeth, and sore joints.

The trip around Cape Horn was dangerous as well as unpleasant. Ferocious rains and freezing gales buffeted the vessels, pushing them toward Antarctica. Some ship captains tried to save time by rounding South America through the Strait of Magellan, but this waterway had raging currents, rip tides, and freakish storms. Even for well-built ships with skilled captains, the Cape Horn voyage was hazardous. During the gold rush days, when rotten ships were sent out with incompetent skippers, wrecks were frighteningly common.

Though shorter than the trip around Cape Horn, the Central American route was just as rough. After a three-week voyage from New York City to Chagres, Panama, the argonauts had to cross the Isthmus of Panama—a narrow strip of land between the Atlantic and Pacific Oceans. For the first leg of the journey, the argonauts hired Panamanians with long canoes, called bungos, to paddle them up the Chagres River. The 40-mile journey—through dense, muggy jungles filled with shrieking parrots and jabbering monkeys—took about three days. When the forty-niners reached Gorgona or Cruces, two villages at the end of the river, they hired native guides to lead them to

The rough passage didn't affect the hopes of the forty-niners. George Payson, after a rough voyage, wrote: "Through storms and thirst, and burning fever, I was sustained by dreams of golden joy…My calculations, so I thought, were by no means extravagant: $2,000 certain—$20,000 probable—$100,000 possible."

Panama City, 20 miles away. On mules and by foot, the gold-rushers traveled over a primitive, narrow trail that twisted through mountains, along cliffs, through streams, and across jungles. The travelers were tormented by mosquitoes, flies, and other insects. They were baked by the sun, drenched by rainstorms, and frightened by poisonous snakes. For overnight stops, the forty-niners rented hammocks in crowded native huts.

Once the gold hunters arrived in Panama City, they often had to wait for weeks or months for a ship to take them to San Francisco. The small number of hotels in Panama City filled up quickly, and the growing crowd of emigrants set up crude camps on the outskirts of town. Thousands became ill with typhoid, dysentery, yellow fever, malaria, and cholera. With few doctors and little medicine, many died. Some men grew impatient waiting for transportation to San Francisco, and hired canoes or fishing boats to take them to California. Most of these craft either returned within a few weeks or were wrecked at sea.

The first vessel to carry argonauts to San Francisco was the steamship *California*. In October 1848, before the gold rush started, the *California* had left New York and headed for San

Francisco. By the time the vessel rounded Cape Horn and reached Panama City—on January 17, 1849—about 1,500 American gold-hunters were waiting to board. However the ship, which had berths for 210 people, was already transporting many South Americans. They had heard of California's gold and boarded when the vessel stopped in Peru. The Americans were furious, and demanded passage to San Francisco. The captain crammed as many Americans on board as possible, and on February 1, the ship steamed away with more than 400 passengers.

Some argonauts slept in the hold; others slept on the dining table, in hammocks hung from the masts, on coils of rope on deck—anywhere they could find a spot. The *California* took about a month to travel the 3,735 miles to San Francisco, arriving on February 28, 1849. The passengers and crew bustled ashore, leaving the ship abandoned.

Little by little, conditions on the Central American route improved. Merchants built hotels and taverns along the Isthmus of Panama, and by 1851 there were plenty of ships traveling up the Pacific Coast.

Ships also came to California from other countries, and by July 1849, vessels were arriving from around the world. By the end of 1849, about 700 ships had docked in San Francisco harbor, bringing more than 40,000 Americans and foreigners. Most of these vessels were deserted by their crews, and the harbor was soon packed with abandoned ships.

👆 Many people set out for California in wagon trains, unaware of the dangerous circumstances that lay ahead. Optimistic pioneers were threatened by harsh weather conditions, unpredictable food and water supplies, disease, and Indian attacks.

OVERLAND ROUTES TO CALIFORNIA

MANY AMERICAN GOLD-RUSHERS, ESPECIALLY FROM THE MIDWEST, TRAVELED TO CALIFORNIA on overland trails. A large number of emigrants took steamships to towns on the Missouri River. Some of these were Independence, Missouri; St. Joseph, Missouri; or Council Bluffs, Iowa. At these sites, the forty-niners joined wagon trains for the roughly 2,000-mile trip—across the central plains, over the Rocky Mountains, past the western desert, and through the Sierra Nevada Mountains—to the California gold fields. Travelers had a choice of routes. Some took the Oregon Trail to Salt Lake City and then went on to California. Others took the Santa Fe Trail to Santa Fe, and trekked to California from there.

Overland trips had to begin in late spring when the grass was tall enough to feed the animals. Journeys could not begin too late however, because early snows sometimes blocked mountain paths. All gold-rushers knew the grisly tale of the Donner party—87 men, women, and children trapped in the Sierra Nevada Mountains during the winter of 1845-46. The Donner group, caught in a pass with no supplies, had to resort to **cannibalism** to stay alive.

Overland travelers enjoyed socializing in the evenings. After supper, the forty-niners gathered around the campfire, told stories, played violins and accordions, played cards, and sang their favorite California songs. The following popular song was sung to the tune of "Oh Susannah."

I come from Massachusetts
With my washbowl on my knee;
I'm going to California
The gold dust for to see.
It rained all night the day I left
The weather it was dry;
The sun so hot I froze to death
Oh brother don't you cry.

Chorus:
I soon shall be in Frisco
And then I'll look around;
And when I see the gold lumps there
I'll pick them off the ground.
I'll scrape the mountain clean, my boys
I'll drain the rivers dry;
A pocketful of rocks bring home
So brother, don't you cry.

Eventually, 47 survivors were brought to California by rescue teams, over what is now called Donner Pass. Thus, forty-niners trekking across the country knew they had only four or five months to reach California.

Prospectors could take railroads part of the journey west, but the longest stretch of travel had to be done in wagons. California would not be linked to the east coast until May 1869, when the transcontinental railroad was completed.

As spring 1849 approached, thousands of emigrants, including women and children traveling with their families, hurried to Independence, St. Joseph, and Council Bluffs. The hotels and boarding houses soon filled, and vast tent communities formed outside the towns. Because of the crowding, diseases spread easily, and cholera claimed many victims.

By the time the wagon trains left, most gold-hunters had loaded up tons of supplies, including furniture, stoves, extra wagon wheels, hammers, anvils, and all kinds of mining

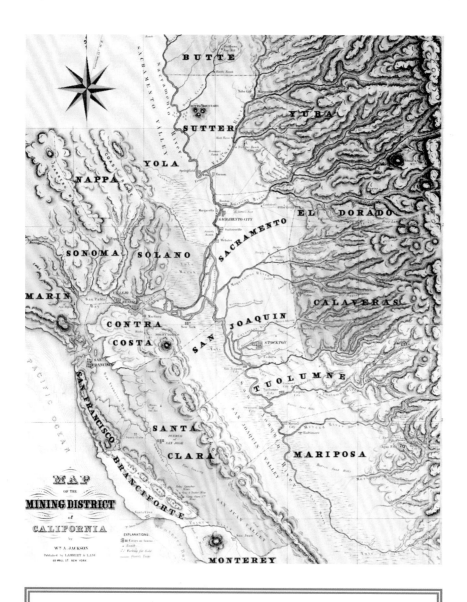

🖐 California's population increased quickly, thanks to the many prospectors and merchants who traveled there in the late 1840s and early 1850s. This 1851 map of the San Francisco Bay area shows both towns and gold camps.

equipment. Forty-niners also carried large quantities of food, including bacon, salt pork, flour, sugar, salt, cornmeal, crackers, rice, beans, coffee, baking soda, and dried fruit. Many of these items, even sacks of food, had to be abandoned during the trip. Luckily, the emigrants were able to supplement their food stores by hunting, fishing, and gathering berries and greens along the trail.

When scouts reported that conditions were favorable, wagon trains began their journey west. Many of the wagons had names and slogans printed on their sides, such as "CALIFORNIA OR BUST," "GOLD HUNTER," "TO THE LAND OF GOLD," or "MEET ME AT SUTTER'S FORT."

Emigrants on the Oregon Trail followed the Platte River across the central plains, past Fort Kearney and Fort Laramie. The forty-niners then traveled along the Sweetwater River, up and over South Pass in the Rocky Mountains, and on to Salt Lake City. Most emigrants then followed the Humboldt River, through the Forty-Mile Desert, to the Humboldt Sink—where the river empties. Finally, the forty-niners crossed the Sierra Nevada Mountains and arrived in the Sacramento Valley, the site of the gold fields.

The overland trip was difficult. Accidents were common, and many forty-niners died. On the plains, heavy storms often swelled the streams, making passage dangerous. Animals and wagons were easily whisked away by rapid currents, and many men died trying to save them. Forty-niners crossing rivers by ferryboat sometimes fell in and drowned. On dry land, emigrants were occasionally thrown from their wagons and crushed under

While wagons and ships headed to California, Rufus Porter, editor of *Scientific American*, designed another means of transportation. He planned to build an "aerial locomotive"—a passenger cabin suspended below an enormous balloon powered by steam engines. Porter said it would attain a speed of 100 miles per hour and reach California in a few days. Though Porter sold advance tickets to many hopeful forty-niners, the aerial locomotive was never built.

the wheels. Moreover, the prairie was flat, with few landmarks, and travelers got hopelessly lost if they wandered far from their wagon train. One of the worst threats to the forty-niners was cholera, which struck often and killed quickly. Many victims were sick for only a few hours before they died. Nevertheless—tortured by gnats and mosquitoes, choked and blinded by dust, and slowed down by muddy trails—the treasure hunters slogged across the plains.

When they finally reached the Sweetwater River, the travelers came across Independence Rock, the best-known landmark on the trail. This huge stone on the north bank of the river had supposedly been named by a party of American fur trappers in 1829. The smooth surfaces of the rock, some as high as 80 feet above the ground, were signed with the names of myriad travelers—fur traders, colonists, missionaries, and forty-niners.

Gold seekers occasionally met Indians along the trail. Most of them were friendly and willing to trade, but they resented forty-niners slaying bison and other animals on tribal land and sometimes stole emigrants' horses and oxen.

When emigrants finally got over the Rocky Mountains, they came to a wide desert. The fiery heat sapped the strength of the animals, and the mules struggled to pull the wagons. To lighten the load, forty-niners threw out most of their belongings. Water became hard to find and dust covered everything, adding to the travelers' misery. Graves of treasure hunters and skeletons of oxen, horses, and mules were strewn along the path. In fact, many travelers, wagons, and animals never made it to California. They either turned back or died along the way.

Margaret Frink, an overland traveler, wrote the following about crossing the desert: "For many weeks we had been accustomed to see property abandoned and animals dead or dying. But those scenes were here doubled and trebled. Horses, mules, and oxen, suffering from heat, thirst, and starvation, staggered along until they fell and died…Both sides of the road for miles were lined with dead animals and abandoned wagons."

The final barrier before reaching the gold fields was the snow-capped Sierra Nevada range. The climb up the mountains was long and hard. The gold seekers had to cross freezing streams and narrow trails littered with boulders. Even the descent was treacherous. The mountains were so steep in places that wagons had to be lowered with ropes. Moreover, early winters sometimes brought bitter weather before the emigrants finally reached the gold fields. Though the trip was difficult, more than 40,000 overland travelers made their way to California during 1949 alone.

Miners used several techniques to find gold. From the simple method of panning a river to more complex techniques involving sluices, "long toms," and other equipment, the forty-niners were willing to try anything they thought might help them strike it rich.

MINING AND MINING TOWNS

BY THE END OF 1849, MINERS THROUGHOUT THE FOOTHILLS OF THE SIERRA NEVADA Mountains were collecting **placer** (rhymes with passer) **gold**—loose particles of gold mixed with sand and pebbles. California's gold formed eons ago, when seething underground waters flowed into cracks in rock formations. The waters cooled to form gold-rich quartz veins, called the **Mother Lode**. Over time, mountains containing the Mother Lode were eroded by rain and wind, freeing tons of gold fragments. The fragments, carried away by flowing water, formed placer gold in the gullies, creeks, streams, rivers, sandbars, and hills of the Sacramento Valley.

Forty-niners scrambled all over central California, especially gold-laden waterways such as the Feather, Bear, and American Rivers, all of which flow into the Sacramento River, and the Cosumnes, Mokelumne, Calaveras, Stanislaus, Tuolomne, and Merced Rivers, which flow into the San Joaquin River. Mining camps sprang up everywhere. There were hundreds of them, with names like Squabbletown, Chucklehead Diggings, Mad Ox Ravine, Frenchman's Flat, Git-Up-And-Git, Rattlesnake Bar, and Cut Throat.

Amazing tales spread from California—about rivers strewn with gold nuggets as big as chicken eggs, and streams paved with gold—but they were not true. Occasionally, a miner might find a hefty gold nugget or a crevice filled with gold particles, but most forty-niners toiled from dawn to dusk, in icy rivers formed from melted snow, to collect a few ounces of gold dust.

Miners were restless, and if they did not find gold quickly, they pulled up stakes and hurried to another spot. Gossip about a rich strike sent miners rushing down canyons and across rivers to the likely site. Thus, most "mining towns" were makeshift affairs, composed of tents and simple log structures.

Often, three or four miners lived together in a tent. They took turns chopping wood, making fires, carrying water, cooking, and so on. To shop for food, forty-niners went to a large town once a week. They purchased bacon, beans, flour, rice, salt pork, coffee, dried apples, molasses, sugar, and baking soda. Many miners supplemented their diet by hunting and fishing, and some ate acorns and greens found in the hills. In some camps, Mexican women sold food, like tortillas and frijoles (beans), to the miners.

Mining towns were crowded and dirty. Gold-hunters had little opportunity to take baths, cut their hair, or wash their clothes, and were plagued by fleas and lice. Moreover, injuries and illnesses were common in the gold fields. Forty-niners were racked by backaches, sore hands and feet, dysentery, inflamed joints, malaria, diarrhea, coughs, chills, fevers, and aching muscles. Many miners also got scurvy, from lack of fresh fruits and vegetables. Doctors were scarce, medicine was expensive, and many miners died from lack of medical care. Dead miners were usually wrapped in a blanket and buried in a hole.

Mining season was controlled by California's weather. The summers were too hot and the winters too cold and rainy for digging. The best mining times were spring and fall. During the off-season, most forty-niners migrated to cities, like Coloma, Stockton, Sacramento, or San Francisco. There, restaurants, saloons, gambling houses, general stores, and boarding houses were lined up, anxious to serve the miners' needs. Successful miners liked to spend their money, and freely bought champagne, fine liquors, expensive foods, and other frills.

Prices in mining areas were very high. A jar of pickles and two sweet potatoes cost $11, a needle and thread went for $7.50, onions were $2 each, eggs were $3 apiece, and a barrel of flour cost $800.

When goods were purchased, gold dust or cash (acquired by selling gold) had to be paid at once. A pinch of gold was worth $1, an ounce was worth $16, a small glass of gold was

Work of the Miner

Forty-niners used a variety of procedures and equipment to mine placer deposits, including **panning**, **rockers**, **long toms**, tunneling, and coyote hole mining.

To pan for gold, a miner crouched at the edge of a waterway, or stood in the freezing water, and dug up a pan full of dirt and water. He then tipped the pan while swirling the contents, so that the sand and water spilled out, leaving the gold—which is heavier than sand—on the bottom. Miners could work about five pans of dirt per hour.

Some gold-hunters used rockers, which could handle more dirt than pans. A rocker looked like an open-ended baby cradle with a grate on top. A miner put a shovelful of muddy sand on the grate, then rocked the cradle while pouring water over the dirt. Large stones rolled off, while sand and gold dust fell through the grate's holes. Strips of wood on the bottom of the rocker, called **riffles**, caught gold dust as sand and water ran out of the cradle's open end. Using a cradle was hard work, so two miners often formed partnerships to operate them together.

By 1851, an apparatus called a long tom was in common use. This was a wooden trough, from 12 to 25 feet long, with a grate at the end. Under the grate was a riffle box, like the bottom of a rocker. The long tom was set at a slant and

worth $100, and a large glassful was worth $1,000. In gold rush California, merchants did exceptionally well, making far more money than most miners.

Forty-niners relaxed when they could. When weather conditions prevented mining, gold-hunters enjoyed card positioned so that water ran through it constantly. Miners shoveled dirt into the long tom, which was washed through the trough and across the grate. As in a rocker, small particles dropped through the grate's holes, and gold dust was trapped in the riffle box as sand flowed out. Small long toms could be operated by one or two men, while longer ones were worked by six or eight men.

Some forty-niners tunneled into hillsides to find gold. To locate gold in hills, miners sometimes used devices like divining rods—forked branches that supposedly twitched near gold, or gold magnets—metal boxes thought to give off electric shocks when gold was near. After a spot was chosen, miners used picks and shovels to tunnel into the hill's side. As the tunnel widened and deepened, the miners shored it up with boards to prevent collapse. Though tunneling sometimes uncovered rich gold deposits, it was very dangerous. Cave-ins were common, and gold-seekers were sometimes buried alive.

Some gold-miners dug coyote holes, or deep shafts in the ground, to find gold. Coyote hole mining required at least two men working together—one digging at the bottom of the hole, the other pulling up the dirt with a bucket and rope. Though miners shored up the pits as they dug, cave-ins were common, and many gold-hunters were crushed by collapsing holes.

games, bowling, gambling, billiards, chess, wrestling matches, boxing matches, foot races, shows, and other amusements. Miners also enjoyed dances, but women were scarce in the early years of the gold rush, so the men danced with each other.

To entertain themselves after a long day at the mines, prospectors held miners balls. Since there were few women in mining camps, the prospectors usually had to dance with each other. It was common for one dancer to wear an apron; this man would follow the female steps of the dance.

Sporting activities of Californios were especially popular with forty-niners, and miners flocked to horse races, cockfights, bullfights, and bull-and-bear fights—spectacles in which grizzly bears were placed in arenas to fight bulls. These exhibitions attracted many spectators, who bet on the outcome.

By the early 1850s, roads to the West Coast were well established, and professional entertainers flocked to California.

The Spider Dance

Lola Montez, a world-famous dancer, traveled to California in 1853. Her best-known act was the "spider dance," in which she pretended to stray into a nest of spiders, which crawled into her petticoats. Montez then whirled around the stage, shaking out the "spiders," which were made of cork, rubber, and whalebone.

Montez bought a home in Grass Valley, California, and became friendly with a boardinghouse owner named Mary Ann Crabtree, and her six-year-old daughter, Lotta. Montez gave Lotta Crabtree singing and dancing lessons, and the little girl went on to become a popular entertainer. When Lotta performed for audiences in mining towns, the enthusiastic miners threw gold coins and nuggets on the stage.

Cities and large mining towns had theaters featuring comedy acts, singers, Shakespearean plays, variety acts, minstrel shows, circuses, concerts, and other entertainments.

Though most forty-niners barely found enough gold to cover their expenses, some miners struck it rich. One southern man and his slave were digging in Old Dry Diggings, near Coloma. The slave kept dreaming about finding gold under a certain cabin in the camp. When the southerner had the same dream, he bought the cabin. Together, the two men dug up the cabin's dirt floor and panned out $20,000 in gold.

When another forty-niner died near Carson Creek, his companions wanted to give him a proper burial. One of

W. H. Jackson, a famous western photographer, painted this scene of hydraulic mining around 1865. In the distance on the right, a group of men are directing a high-pressure stream of water at the side of a mountain. The men with picks and shovels are sifting through the muck looking for gold deposits. This method was used to mine gold after the placer deposits were depleted.

them, a former preacher, prayed while the other miners knelt around the grave. As they listened to the sermon, the miners picked up dirt from the grave and ran it through their fingers. Suddenly, one of them yelled, "Color," a miner's term for gold. The preacher quickly ended the funeral, the body was removed from the grave, and the preacher and congregation began digging for gold.

One of the most famous stories about the gold fields involves a miner named Thomas Stoddard. In the winter of 1849, Stoddard staggered into a mining camp on the Feather River. Stoddard claimed that he and a friend were prospecting in the hills, and found a lake carpeted with chunks of gold. According to Stoddard, he collected

Incredible finds were sometimes made in the California gold fields. The Calaveras Nugget, found at Carson Hill in 1854, weighed 195 troy pounds. It was worth $43,534.

some of the gold and headed back to his camp, but got lost and was attacked by Indians. During the clash, Stoddard lost his gold and his companion. He then wandered around until he came to the mining camp on the Feather River.

This story excited the miners in the camp, and they provided Stoddard with food and shelter through the winter. In the spring, a group of miners paid Stoddard a fee to take them to "Gold Lake," and Stoddard guided them into the mountains. By then, rumors of the fabulous lake had spread, and other forty-niners followed behind, hoping to strike it rich. For six days, Stoddard led the gold-hunters on a futile trek through the mountains. The miners grew suspicious, thinking Stoddard had cheated them. They threatened to hang Stoddard if he did not find the lake

 John C. Frémont was an American soldier and explorer. He gained national fame, and the nickname "the Pathfinder," for his expeditions through the American West in the 1840s. By a stroke of luck, he became rich during the Gold Rush when gold was discovered on his property in California. Fremont later was a presidential candidate in 1856 and a Union general during the Civil War. He lost most of his Gold Rush wealth in bad investments during the late 1860s.

within a day. That night, Stoddard stole away while the other miners were asleep.

When the forty-niners woke up and found Stoddard gone, they returned to their camps. Three Germans in the expedition took a roundabout route back, digging as they went. By luck, one of them found a group of rocks, the cracks of which were packed with gold. The Germans dug the gold out with their knives, and in four days had collected $36,000 worth. News of the strike spread quickly, and thousands of miners swarmed into the area. The site had enormous reserves of gold, and came to be known as Rich Bar.

Another lucky man was John C. Frémont, a well-known army officer and explorer who lived in California. In 1847, Frémont gave his business agent, Thomas Larkin, $3,000 to buy a section of land south of San Francisco. Instead, Larkin mistakenly purchased 45,000 acres in the Sierra foothills— which made Frémont furious. A few years later, however, Frémont was thrilled to find that his property, named Rancho de las Mariposas, contained an enormous amount of gold.

By the 1850's, most of California's rich placer gold was gone, and gold-seekers were forced to work poorer deposits. To keep mining profitable, vast quantities of dirt had to be rinsed. Because great amounts of water were needed, channels were built to bring water to the mine fields. This was expensive, so gold mining was eventually taken over by big companies with numerous employees.

Mining companies also began working the Mother Lode— the gold-rich quartz veins in the mountains. This operation required many men and much machinery to blast rocks loose, transport them to ore refineries, crush them to powder, and extract the gold flakes.

FIAT JUSTITIA RUAT CŒLUM

COMMITTEE OF VIGILANCE SAN FRANCISCO

NO PARTY. NO CREED. NO SECTIONAL ISSUES

As California's population increased, so did the crime level. In cities like San Francisco, tough gangs of criminals threatened to take over until lawmen stepped in—or angry citizens took the law into their own hands. To ensure order, vigilance committees were established.

CRIME AND JUSTICE

IN THE EARLY DAYS OF THE GOLD RUSH, THERE
WAS ALMOST NO CRIME IN THE DIGGINGS. FORTY-
niners could leave equipment, food, and sacks of gold in their
tents with little fear of theft. As more and more miners arrived,
however, crime increased.

Since there were no police, the miners created their own
system of justice. When a crime was discovered and a suspect
caught, a miners' meeting would be called. A trial was held,
and a judgment passed down. Since there were no jails to hold
criminals, the verdict was swiftly carried out. Petty thieves
were whipped, and sometimes their ears were cut off to mark
them as robbers. Criminals that murdered or stole large
amounts of property were hanged.

The forty-niners also made laws regulating mining.
A person was allowed to claim a reasonable-size plot to
mine, which varied from 10 to 50 square feet, depending on
the richness of the diggings. The claim had to be marked
and boundaries staked. Each miner could hold only one
claim at a time, and the miner had to work his claim at least
once a week or he lost it. Moreover, a miner could not rent
his claim to others. If arguments arose about who had the

right to a claim, a miners' jury was chosen. The jury heard witnesses and then determined the owner.

With no police force in California's cities, criminals from all over the world flocked to San Francisco. There, they could commit their crimes with little fear of punishment.

One San Francisco criminal gang was called the Hounds. Most Hounds were soldiers from a New York regiment called Stevenson's Volunteers that had come to California during the Mexican War in 1846, and stayed on. The Hounds took merchandise from stores without paying, and demanded free food and drinks in restaurants. They attacked merchants who did not give in to their demands. The Hounds disliked foreigners, and decided to drive Chilenos (people from Chile) out of San Francisco. On July 15, 1849, the Hounds raided the Chileno camps, setting fire to the tents and beating the residents.

Other San Franciscans, afraid the Hounds would trash more of the city, decided to stop them. Honest citizens rounded up the Hounds and put them on trial. The Hounds' leader was sentenced to 10 years in prison, and other gang members were given lesser terms. There were no jails, so the culprits were not actually imprisoned. The gang members were thoroughly frightened, however, and never caused trouble again.

One of the worst outlaw bands in San Francisco was a group of Australians, called the Sydney Ducks. They had settled in a part of the city that came to be called Sydney Town. Whenever the gang started trouble, people said, "The Sydney Ducks are cackling."

☛ Drunken prospectors were easy targets for con men during the California Gold Rush. In this 19th century illustration, two miners fight over a card game in a gold panning camp.

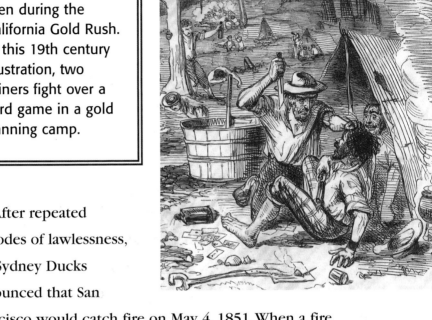

After repeated episodes of lawlessness, the Sydney Ducks announced that San Francisco would catch fire on May 4, 1851. When a fire actually broke out on that day, the Sydney Ducks looted offices, stores, and homes, carrying off everything they could. San Francisco residents were angry. They formed a "committee of vigilance" containing 180 men. The **vigilantes** soon captured, tried, and hanged four Sydney Ducks, and ordered others to leave town, breaking the power of the gang.

As cities and camps grew, more traditional administrations were formed. At first, many settlements elected **alcaldes**, whose duties combined those of mayor and judge. Eventually, prisons were built in California, and trained law enforcement officers, rather than citizens' groups, vigilantes, and alcaldes, became responsible for administering justice.

👆 Chinese workers look for gold by a mountain stream. The man at left with the shovel is wearing a broad-brimmed hat common to the Chinese, sometimes called a coolie hat. American prospectors often discriminated against the Chinese and other foreigner workers.

6

THE RIGHT TO WORK THE GOLD FIELDS

MANY MINERS FROM THE UNITED STATES THOUGHT CALIFORNIA'S GOLD SHOULD BE reserved for "white Americans." They resented and abused Indians and gold-seekers from other countries.

The Native Americans suffered most. California Indians were primitive, peaceful people who lived by hunting, fishing, and gathering plants. Unfortunately, their lands were either in the gold fields or on the road to them. Thus, white gold-seekers, anxious to strike it rich, did not hesitate to force the Native Americans from their homes.

In the mining towns and gold-fields themselves, Indians were treated with scorn. Miners forced the Native Americans to give up their claims, and shot them if they refused. Americans also cheated Indians. Mining companies paid Indians low wages to work in the gold fields, and merchants charged Indians exorbitant prices for goods, like a pound of gold for a pound of raisins.

Two groups, one American and one French, laid claim to a plot of land in the gold-rich area called Rich Bar. The two sets of miners agreed to settle the matter with a fistfight between one man from each side. After a three-hour battle, the American won, and the French group moved to another spot. That spot, called French Gulch, turned out to be the richest of the diggings around Rich Bar.

In addition to displacing Indians, American miners tried to drive off gold-seekers from other countries. To do this, Americans created mining districts that barred foreigners. Moreover, in 1850, the California Legislature passed a Foreign Miners Tax, which charged foreign gold-hunters $20 a month—an amount many could not pay. Because of the harassment, some foreigners simply left the mines. Others established their own camps, in non-white districts.

Americans especially disliked Hispanics, for several reasons. Bad feelings remained from the Mexican War; Hispanics had dark skin and spoke Spanish; and gold-hunters from Mexico, Chile, and Peru were experienced miners who did well in the gold fields. Thus, if the Foreign Miners Tax did not drive off Hispanics, Americans tried to run them off by force. This unfair treatment prompted some Hispanics to become bandits.

The most famous bandit in the gold fields was the Mexican-American outlaw Joaquin Murrieta. Early in the gold rush, Murrieta was mining in the Stanislaus River region when a band of thugs raided his camp, stole his gold, and attacked his wife. To get revenge, Murrieta assembled a gang of bandits, including Manuel Garcia, also known as Three-Fingered-Jack. Murrieta's outlaw band robbed and killed white miners in camps, ranches, and towns throughout California.

The California Legislature was determined to get rid of Murrieta. In 1853, it authorized Captain Harry Love to put together a group of rangers to stop the bandit. Love's troops caught up with Murrieta's gang in the Tulare Valley, killing Murrieta and Three-Fingered-Jack. Captain Love cut off Murrieta's head and the hand of Three-Fingered-Jack, preserved them in jars of alcohol, and put them on public display.

HEAD OF A CALIFORNIA NATIVE MALE INDIAN.

Chinese **immigrants** experienced some of the worst discrimination in the mining region. By

Prospectors headed west sometimes called California an uninhabited region. This was not true, of course; many California Indians had been living on the land for hundreds of years. This drawing was made in the early 19th century, as part of a study of the native people of California.

Some of the people drawn to California were Jewish gold-hunters and merchants. Among them was Levi Strauss, a merchant who went to San Francisco to sell dry goods to miners. Noticing the forty-niners' need for durable clothing, Strauss designed sturdy pants, eventually made from blue denim, with the seams reinforced by small copper rivets. These blue jeans, also called Levi's, became popular with gold miners, cowboys, and working people all over the world.

1852, at least 20,000 Chinese were living in California, and more continued to arrive. Though Chinese people took many kinds of jobs—as laborers, waiters, cooks, launderers, merchants, and servants—most became miners. Many mining settlements had "Chinatowns," where Chinese people followed their own customs. Americans thought Chinese people looked odd—with their long "pigtails" (queues) and the blue blouses and loose trousers worn in their homeland. Americans also resented the fact that Chinese miners, by working hard, could extract gold from claims abandoned by whites.

The State of California passed laws that barred Chinese from becoming citizens. The Chinese were not allowed to own real estate or to open businesses. In addition, whites harassed and cheated Chinese people, and drove Chinese miners away from promising claims.

African-Americans also experienced prejudice in the gold fields. Several thousand blacks were living in California

by 1852. Some were free blacks, and others were brought
into the area as slaves. Some free blacks became miners,
while others worked in cities, as cooks, waiters, stewards,
porters, barbers, mechanics, and businessmen. African-
Americans had few rights, however, and were not allowed to
vote or testify against whites until 1863. Also, although
slavery was illegal in California, the state legislature passed
the Fugitive Slave Act in 1852. This law guaranteed that slave
owners could capture slaves that had escaped to California
and take them home.

👆 This view of riverboats moored in Sacramento was made around 1850. Immigrants traveled from all points of the globe with the hope of starting a new life of freedom and fortune in America.

7

SETTLING CALIFORNIA

SEVERAL CALIFORNIA TOWNS, INCLUDING SAN FRANCISCO, SACRAMENTO, AND STOCKTON, GREW into large cities during the gold rush. In January 1848, when gold was discovered at Sutter's Fort, San Francisco had about 900 residents. By October 1849, the city had a population of 25,000, and was growing rapidly. All kinds of people made their way west, including miners, merchants, businessmen, doctors, lawyers, preachers, barbers, blacksmiths, politicians, and saloon keepers.

San Francisco grew so fast that there was no time to construct buildings. The city was composed of tents, flimsy shacks, and abandoned ships hauled on shore and used as stores and boardinghouses. Because of this, fires started easily. There were at least six disastrous blazes during the early years of the gold rush. One of the worst fires, on May 3, 1851, burned for 10 hours. It destroyed 2,000 homes and much of San Francisco's business district.

A major disadvantage of living in San Francisco was mud. During California's rainy season, San Francisco was covered with sticky black mud. Dogs and drunks sometimes drowned in the muck, and horses occasionally sank so deep

The forty-niners added popular phrases to the English language, like: "I hope it pans out," "staking a claim," and "hitting pay dirt."

they could not be rescued. The huge number of mudholes made some streets impassable. San Francisco residents filled the deepest cavities with boxes, trunks, cases, debris, and rotting food—just so pedestrians could walk over them. Still, people's boots and clothes became covered with stinking mud.

Over time, the tents, shacks, and muddy streets of San Francisco were replaced by brick buildings and sidewalks, and the city became a modern, thriving **metropolis**.

At the beginning of the gold rush, few women made the long, hazardous journey west. By the early-1850's, though, many women were traveling to California—to find jobs and husbands. Women ran boardinghouses, restaurants, and laundries, and worked as card dealers, waitresses, librarians, cooks, teachers and entertainers.

When mining companies took over from individual miners, the gold rush began to wind down. Then, in 1859, silver was discovered in Nevada. **Prospectors** rushed to the new treasure fields, and the California gold rush ended.

Historians consider the gold rush one of the most important events in American history. It made the United States a leading gold producer, sped up settlement of the Far

West, added a new state to the Union, and hastened the building of the **Transcontinental Railroad**, completed on May 10, 1869.

The conclusion of the gold rush did not put an end to California's growth. Many miners left, but hundreds of thousands of people stayed. California became a wealthy farming state, with cattle ranches, fisheries, forests, oil, other minerals, wineries, manufacturing, shipping, banking, and technology contributing to its riches.

GLOSSARY

Alcalde

The person who was elected to preside over a mining settlement; the position included the duties of mayor and judge.

Argonaut

A voyager on a ship; those who moved the California by ship were called Argonauts.

Californios

Mexican people who had been living in California for generations before the gold rush.

Cholera

A disease marked by severe vomiting and diarrhea that affected many gold-seekers as they headed toward California.

Cannibalism

The eating of human flesh by another human being.

Dredge

A machine used for removing earth, often with either buckets on an endless chain or a suction tube.

Emigrant

A person who leaves one place to settle elsewhere.

Forty-niner

A person who headed to California to find gold; they were named after the year in which the biggest portion of the gold rush took place, 1849.

Immigrant

A person who comes from another country to settle in a new land.

Long Tom

A long, wooden trough with a grate at one end that was set at an angle so that water ran through it to separate gold from sand, rocks, and other sediment.

Metropolis

A large city, especially one that is among the most important cities in its region.

Mother Lode

Cracks in quartz formations that contained rich supplies of gold.

Panning

The act of swirling a mixture of water and dirt in a pan to separate the heavier gold particles.

Placer Gold

Loose particles of gold that were found among sand and small pebbles.

Prospector

A person who explores for a valuable mineral, such as gold.

Riffles

Strips of wood in various mining devices that caught gold particles while letting other elements, such as sand and water, pass through.

Rocker

A device that uses a rocking motion to force small particles of sand and gold dust into a grate, where riffles caught the gold and let the sand and water pass through.

Scurvy

A disease caused by lack of vitamin C that attacks muscles and joints, eventually causing death.

Tailrace

A channel that carries water away from a mill.

Transcontinental Railroad

A rail line that connected the East and West in the United States, thus improving movement of people and cargo across the country.

Vigilante

A person who takes the law into his or her own hands; someone who makes an effort to enforce laws on their own.

TIMELINE

1839

John Sutter acquires 50,000 acres of land in California's central valley and begins to build a ranch, called New Helvetia (Sutter's Fort).

1846

The Mexican War breaks out between the United States and Mexico.

1848

James Marshall discovers gold at Sutter's Mill in New Helvetia on January 24; the Treaty of Guadalupe Hidalgo ends the Mexican War on February 2 and makes California a territory of the United States; *The Californian* publishes the first article about the discovery of gold in California on March 15; Sam Brannan goes to San Francisco on May 12 to announce that gold has been discovered in the American River; residents of San Francisco race to the gold fields; The *New York Herald* newspaper publishes an article about the discovery of gold in California; President James Polk tells Congress that California has extensive gold deposits, and the gold rush begins.

1849

About 90,000 gold seekers arrive in California.

1850

The discovery of gold-bearing quartz veins in the mountains leads to the development of hard rock mining, which continues for more than 100 years; California becomes the 31st state.

1851

An Australian gang called the Sydney Ducks sets fire to San Francisco and loots the city; vigilantes capture, try, and hang four Sydney Ducks and order others to leave town.

1852

California's gold production reaches about $81 million per year.

1853

Captain Henry Love captures Joaquin Murrieta, the most notorious bandit in the gold fields.

1854

Sacramento becomes the capital of the state of California.

1855

The rich surface placer deposits of California are largely exhausted; mining companies begin working poorer placer deposits; the gold rush begins to wind down.

1859

Silver is discovered in Nevada; prospectors hurry off to work the silver deposits, ending the gold rush.

FURTHER READING

Blake, Arthur, and Pamela Dailey. *The Gold Rush of 1849: Staking a Claim in California*. Brookfield, Conn.: The Millbrook Press, 1995.

Boessenecker, John. *Gold Dust and Gunsmoke: Tales of Gold Rush Outlaws, Gunfighters, Lawmen, and Vigilantes*. New York: John Wiley and Sons, 1999.

Ito, Tom. *The California Gold Rush*. San Diego: Lucent Books, 1997.

Johnson, Susan Lee. *Roaring Camp: The Social World of the California Gold Rush*. New York: W. W. Norton and Company, 2000.

Levy, Jo Ann. *They Saw the Elephant: Women in the California Gold Rush*. Hamden, Conn.: Archon Books, 1990.

Stiles, T. J., ed. *In Their Own Words: Warriors and Pioneers*. New York: The Berkley Publishing Group, 1996.

INTERNET RESOURCES

History of the California Gold Rush
http://www.calgoldrush.com/
http://www.notfrisco.com/calmem/goldrush/index.html.
http://www0.mercurycenter.com/archives/goldrush/

Information about important Gold Rush sites
http://www.goldrush1849.com/

Women in the Gold Rush
http://www.goldrush.com/~joann/

John Sutter describes the discovery of gold
http://www.sfmuseum.org/hist2/gold.html

INDEX

PHOTO CREDITS

ABOUT THE AUTHOR

Dr. Barbara Saffer, a former college instructor, holds Ph.D. degrees in biology and geology. She has written numerous books for young people about science, geography, exploration, and the American West. She lives in Birmingham, Alabama, with her family.